The Well Rounded ENTJ
Find More Harmony, Improve Relationships and Thrive as a Natural Leader

The Ultimate Guide To The ENTJ Personality Type

Use Your Natural Talents and Personality Traits To Succeed
In Your Career, Relationships, and Purpose In Life.

Dan Johnston

Cover Design by Scientist X Designs

www.DreamsAroundTheWorld.com

CONTENTS

WHY YOU SHOULD READ THIS BOOK

Do you know those people for whom everything just seems easy?

Their career or business is always getting better. Their relationships appear happy and fulfilling. They have a satisfying home life, work life and, by damn, never seem to have a complaint in the world. **Let's call these people the "Thrivers".**

Then there are those for whom life feels like a constant upward swim. At work, they feel like they don't belong. Their relationships are either problematic or unsatisfying. To them life has always been a struggle. Let's call them the strugglers.

What's going on here? Are some of us just blessed with good fortune? Is everyone else just cursed with constant struggle?

Don't worry; there are no magical forces at work – just some psychology. It's been my experience that there is only one difference between the Strugglers and the Thrivers.

The Thrivers, by reflection, study, or just dumb luck, have built their lives around their natural personalities. Their work utilizes their strengths while their relationships complement their weaknesses.

A small percentage of the Thrivers came into their lives "naturally". The careers their parents or teachers recommended were the perfect fit for them, or they had a gut feeling that turned out to be right. They met their ideal partner who complemented them perfectly. I believe, however, that this group is the minority.

Most Thrivers have spent years "watching" themselves and reflecting about who they really are. For some this is a natural process, for others (myself included) it's a more deliberate process. We read, studied, questioned and took tests all in the name of self-awareness. We've made it a priority to know and understand ourselves.

Whatever a Thriver learns about themselves, they use to make significant changes in their life. They change careers, end relationships and start new hobbies. They do all this so that one day their life will be fulfilling and have a natural flow to it: a life in which they can thrive.

This book is for Thrivers: Past, present and future.

If you once had your flow but can't seem to find it again, read on.

If you're in your flow and want to keep and improve it, read on.

And if you're one of the beautiful souls struggling but committed to finding your flow and thriving, you're in the right place. Read on.

Today you may feel like a salmon swimming upstream, but this is a temporary state of being. One day soon, you will find yourself evolving. Perhaps into a dolphin, swimming amongst those with whom you belong, free to be yourself, to play and to enjoy life. Maybe you'd rather find your place as a whale - wise and powerful, roaming the oceans and setting your own path, respected and admired by all.

KNOWLEDGE BRINGS AWARENESS AND AWARENESS BRINGS SUCCESS

I'm an entrepreneur as well as a writer. As an entrepreneur, negotiation plays a big part in any success I might have. One of the secrets to being a good negotiator is to always be the one with the most information in the room. The same holds true for decision making in our personal lives.

When it comes to the big things in life, we can't make a good decision if we don't have all the relevant information.

I think most of us understand this on an external level. When we're shopping for a new car, we research our options: the prices, the engines, and the warranties. We find out as much as we can to help make our decision.

Unfortunately, we often forget the most important factor in our decisions: Us.

A Ford Focus is a better economic decision and a more enjoyable drive than a SUV...but that doesn't matter if you're 7 feet tall or have 5 kids who need to be driven to Hockey in the snow.

When it comes to life decisions, such as our work or relationships, who we are is the most important decision factor.

It doesn't matter if all your friends say he is the perfect guy...it only matters if he's perfect for you. It doesn't matter if your family wants you to be a lawyer, a doctor or an accountant…what do you want to do? If you make your decision based on what the outside world says, you won't find the levels of happiness or fulfillment you desire.

In order to make the best decisions for you, you must first know yourself. That is the purpose of this book: To provide the most in-depth information on the ENTJ personality type available anywhere.

By Reading This Book You Will:

- Improve self-awareness.
- Uncover your natural strengths.

- Understand your weaknesses.
- Discover new career opportunities.
- Learn how to have better relationships.
- Develop a greater understanding of your family, partner and friends.
- Have the knowledge to build your ideal life around your natural personality.
- Have more happiness, health, love, money and all round life success while feeling more focused and fulfilled.

FREE READER-ONLY EXCLUSIVES: WORKBOOK AND BONUSES

When I wrote this book, I set out to create the most *useful* guide available. I know there will always be bigger or more detailed textbooks out there, but how many of them are actually helpful?

To help you get the most from this book I have created a collection of free extras to support you along the way. To download these, simply visit the special section of my website: www.dreamsaroundtheworld.com/thrive

You will be asked to enter your email address so I can send you the "Thriving Bonus Pack". You'll receive:

- A 5-part mini-course (delivered via email) with tips on how to optimize your life so you can maximize your strengths and thrive.
- A compatibility chart showing how you are most likely to relate to the other 15 personality types. You'll discover which people are likely to become good friends (or more) and who you should avoid at all costs.
- A PDF workbook to ramp up the results you'll get from this book. It's formatted to be printed, so you can fill in your answers to the exercises in each chapter as you go.

To download the Thriving Bonus Pack visit:

www.DreamsAroundTheWorld.com/thrive

INTRODUCTION TO THIS SERIES

The goal is this series is to provide a clear window into the strengths, weaknesses, opportunities and challenges of each type.

I want you to have every advantage possible in the areas of work, play, relationships, health and finance.

You'll discover new things about yourself and find new ways to tap into your strengths and create a life where you thrive.

This book is part of a series: each one focuses on one type. You will find I write directly to you, although I do not make an assumption as to your personality type or your traits. I will generally refer to the type, aka ENTJ, instead of saying "you". Not every trait of a type applies to everyone of that type, and we never want to make any assumptions about who you are or your limitations.

I would recommend beginning with your type to learn most about yourself, but don't stop there. Each book focuses on a particular type and will be valuable for that type, as well as family, friends, bosses and colleagues of that type.

Even before writing these books I found myself doing extensive reading on the types of my brother, parents, friends and even dates. In my business I would research the types of my assistants, employees and potential business partners. I found that learning about myself got me 60% of the way, and the other 40% came from learning about the other people in my life.

If you plan to read up on all the different types I suggest looking at my "Collection" books, which include multiple types all in one book for a reduced price. It'll be easier and a better price for you than buying each individual book.

DISCLAIMER

I know this book will serve you in discovering your strengths and building your self-awareness. I have researched and written this book based on years of practical experience including running multiple businesses, talking to dozens of people about their strengths and weaknesses, and applying this knowledge to my own life to discover my strengths and build a business around what I do best. With that said, I must emphasize that I am not a psychologist, psychiatrist or counselor, or in any way qualified to offer medical advice. The information in this book is intended to improve your life but it does not replace professional advice in any way and is not legal, medical or psychiatric advice. So, if you're in a bad place or may be suffering from a mental illness please seek professional help!

DISCOVERING THE "EXECUTIVE" PERSONALITY: WHO IS AN ENTJ?

At this point I'm going to assume you're an ENTJ and reading about yourself, or reading about someone you care about who is an ENTJ.

I'm also going to assume you've read some of the basic descriptions online about ENTJs and have bought this book because you want depth and details on how ENTJs can thrive.

So with that, I won't bore you with a drawn out description of ENTJs here. I'll keep it short, and let you get on to the other chapters where we go deeper into specific areas like career and relationships.

ENTJs may be the "Type A" personality if there was one, with "A" standing for accomplishment. ENTJs are disciplined and competitive; they possess a unique blend of social skills, determination, creativity, and logical decision-making. They are goal-oriented, drawn to positions of leadership, and find great enjoyment in creating something new. They also have an excellent understanding of people and one of the most accurate understandings of human nature. This combination of personal values and abilities is one reason ENTJs are so successful as business executives and leaders.

Driven by a desire to grow and to succeed, many ENTJs have an unrelenting energy and determination to reach their goals. They're persistent in their approach and consistent in their decision-making. Most ENTJs would agree with the phrase "slow and steady wins the race"…except for the slow part.

As employers, ENTJs aren't always empathetic or kind, and yet they always strive to be fair and consistent in how they treat people.

They won't sugar coat anything, but they will always strive to be fair, and reward and punish people based on their performance.

ENTJs love a challenge and are always up for taking educated risks. ENTJs are disciplined and excellent money managers. They are great at personal finance and rarely run into trouble. They believe in following the rules and are happy to pay their taxes...even if their share tends to be higher than most other types.

For an ENTJ, life is about achievement, growth, and personal character.

INTRODUCTION TO MYERS BRIGGS

I first discovered Myers Briggs about 5 years ago, although I do have some vague memories of taking a career test in High School. I'm sure that test was likely Myers-Briggs, but who really pays attention to those when you're 16?

Myers-Briggs is one of many options in the world of personality profiles and testing. It is arguably the most popular, and in my opinion it is the best place to start because the results provide insight into all aspects of our lives whereas other tests are often very focused on just career.

Myers-Briggs is based on the idea that we are all different. These differences aren't simply a result of conditioning (as some behavioral psychologists used to argue) but rather a difference in how we're wired.

This doesn't mean that we can't build certain traits, or that any traits are 100% natural. Rather, Myers-Briggs is an opportunity to learn which traits come most naturally to you and which areas you may find challenging or need to invest time in developing.

It's also an opportunity to understand the people around us and get to the root of many conflicts. In fact, understanding the different types and how they relate to others could be the most valuable aspect of Myers-Briggs for many people.

THE 16 TYPES AND FOUR GROUPS

Myers-Briggs includes 16 different personality types that are described by a unique series of 4 letters.

At first, the types appear confusing, but they're really quite simple.

Each type is based on one of two modes of being or thinking for each of the four letters.

- E (extrovert) or I (introvert)
- N (intuitive) or S (sensing)
- T (thinking) or F (feeling)
- P (perceiving) or J (judging)

Now, don't pay too much attention to the words tied to each letter because they don't actually offer a great description for the characteristic.

In just a second I'll share my explanation for each letter. Just before this, I want to share an important point to remember: Personality analysis and profiling is a bit of an art, as well as a science. In other words, since people are so diverse, the descriptions and results aren't always black and white. Some people have a strong preference for one mode or the other, but others are closer to the middle. It's natural for all of us to occasionally feel or demonstrate traits of the other types.

What we want to focus on here is your natural way of being and the functions you are strongest in. It is also important to know that you can, and will, develop your secondary (or auxiliary) and third (or tertiary) "functions" over time and with practice. In doing so, you will create a more balanced personality, with less weak spots, and a more diverse set of skills. In fact, the key to overcoming most personality challenges is to develop your weaker functions.

Generally it's said that we grow our primary function in our early years, our secondary in our twenties and thirties, and our third function some time in our thirties and forties. However, this assumes you're not being proactive and reading a book like this one. In your case, there is no reason you can't leap ahead a few decades and strengthen your other functions ahead of schedule.

WHAT THE FOUR LETTERS MEAN

As you know, there are 4 letters that make up your personality type.

At first these letters can be a little confusing, especially since their descriptions aren't the most telling.

Here's how I explain each letter.

For the first letter in your type, you are either an E, or an I.

The E or I describe how we relate with other people and social situations.

Extroverts are drawn to people, groups, and new social situations. They are generally comfortable at parties and in large groups.

Introverts are more reserved. This is not to say Introverts do now enjoy people, they do. Introverts are just happier in smaller groups, and with people they know and trust like friends or family. Keep in mind, this does not mean that Introverts are not capable of mastering social skills if they must. Rather, they will not be drawn to such situations or find the process as exciting or enjoyable as an extrovert would.

"The Deal Breaker": For some people E or I is obvious. For others the line is blurred. This question will make your preference clear: "Does being around new people or groups add to or drain your energy? If you spent an entire day alone would you feel "off" or bad, or would you be just fine?" If you can spend a day or two alone without feeling bad, or if spending a few hours in a group of people leaves you feeling tired, you're an Introvert.

While Extroverts may often steal a lot of the attention in a room, Introverts often have the upper hand. While many Extroverts crave the spotlight, Introverts are able to sit back and calmly observe, learning more about a situation and making their contributions more meaningful and impactful.

On the other hand, Extroverts have many advantages when it comes to first impressions, wide social circles, and the ability to engage strangers in conversation.

ENTJs are Extroverts. This is why ENTJs enjoy being around people and are so socially skilled within groups or when meeting new people.

For the second letter, you are either an N or an S.

This trait describes how we interact with the world.

Those with the intuitive trait (N) tend to be introspective and imaginative. They enjoy theoretical discussions and "big picture" kind of ideas. For an extreme example, imagine a philosophy professor with a stained suit jacket and a terribly messy office.

Of course, this isn't the reality for most Ns. Most intuitive people live a happy, fulfilled life full of new ideas and inspirations...all while managing the day-to-day aspects of their lives at an acceptable level. Ns have an exceptional imagination and ability to form new ideas, tell stories, and inspire those around them.

Those with the Sensor trait are observant and in touch with their immediate environment. They prefer practical, "hands on" information to theory. They prefer facts over ideas. For an extreme example, think of a mechanic or military strategist.

ENTJs have the intuitive trait. This is why they are drawn to ideas and have a great imagination and pull towards the possibilities.

Third, you are either a T or an F.

This trait describes how you make decisions and come to conclusions, as well as what role emotions play in our personalities and how we deal with them.

Those with the thinker trait are "tough-minded". They tend to be objective and impersonal with others. This can make them appear uncaring, but they are generally very fair. Those with the thinking trait rely on logic and rational arguments for their decisions. The "T" trait would be common amongst (successful) investors and those who need to make impersonal and objective decisions in their careers.

Those with the feeler trait are personal, friendly and sympathetic with others. Their decisions are often influenced by their emotions or the "people" part of a situation. They are also more sensitive and impacted by their emotions, and less afraid to show their emotions to the outside world. The "F" trait would be common amongst counselors and psychologists.

ENTJs have the thinker trait. This is why ENTJs can be so logical. It is also why ENTJs may have trouble empathizing or connecting with more emotional people.

Lastly, you are either a P or a J.

This trait describes how we organize information in our internal and external worlds. This translates into how we schedule ourselves, stay organized, and evaluate our options.

Perceivers are best described as "Probers" or "Explorers". They look for options, opportunities and alternatives; this means they tend to be more creative, open minded and, well, often have messy bedrooms. They're happy to give one plan a try without all the details, knowing they can adjust or try something else in the future.

Judgers are structured and organized. They tend to be more consistent and scheduled. Spreadsheets may be their friends and their rooms will be clean...or at least organized. They prefer concrete plans and closure over openness and possibilities.

You would find more Ps amongst artists and creative groups, whereas professions like accountants and engineers would be almost exclusively Js.

ENTJs have the judging trait. This is one reason they are able to stay organized, focused and disciplined while working towards a goal. Of those with the Judging trait, ENTJs are a bit of an exception and are often very creative and open to new ideas...as long as they see them as realistic options.

THE FOUR GROUPS

Since the original creation of the 16 types, Psychologists have recognized 4 distinct groups, each containing 4 types. The 4 types within each group have distinct traits in common based on sharing 2 of the 4 traits.

The 4 types are:

- The Artisans (The SPs)
- The Guardians (The SJs)
- The Idealists (The NFs)

- The Rationals (The NTs)

As an ENTJ you are a Rational.

Rationals greatest strength is strategy. They are intellectual in speech, and utilitarian in how they pursue their goals.

They are seekers of knowledge and trust reason and logic over emotions and feelings. They seek to gain as much information as possible and apply this knowledge towards long term plans for achieving their goals.

Not known for their empathy, Rationals are considered tough minded in how they deal with others. The truth is, Rationals strive to be honest and fair in their decision making and how they treat people. So even though they may come off as cold or uncaring, their actual decisions are usually very fair and objective.

The Other 3 Rational Types, Your Cousins, Are:

- The Charming Visionary: ENTPs
- The Thinker and Architect: INTPs
- The Strategic Mastermind: INTJs

To learn more about how all the types relate and interact, download the free compatibility chart at:

www.DreamsAroundTheWorld.com/thrive

IN GOOD COMPANY: FAMOUS ENTJS

As an ENTJ, you are amongst some very good company. In this chapter you'll find a collection of famous and "successful" people who are either confirmed, or suspected, as being ENTJs.

Do not use this chapter as a guide to what you must do or who you must be like. Rather, use this chapter as a source of inspiration. It is a chance to see what's possible as an ENTJ and what great things have been accomplished by those who share a similar makeup to you.

Personally, I have found great value in studying famous people from my own type including reading their autobiographies. Most of us spend the early years of our lives feeling lost and trying to figure out our purpose or how we want to end up. I've found studying those of my type who have found their purpose, and then success, gives me a shortcut to understanding my own potential and the directions my life could go.

FAMOUS ENTJS

Actors and Performers
- George Clooney
- David Letterman
- Charlize Theron
- Matt Damon
- Tea Leoni
- Adele
- Cobie Smulders
- Penn Jilette (Penn and Teller)
- Katharine Hepburn

Politicians and Business Leaders
- Napoleon Bonaparte
- Julius Caesar
- Aristotle
- Margaret Thatcher
- Aung San Suu Kyi
- Carl Sagan
- Dick Cheney
- Al Gore
- Madeleine Albright
- Bill Gates

- Rahm Emanuel
- Karl Rove
- Peter Thiel
- Alexander Hamilton
- Rush Limbaugh
- Jack Welch
- Joseph Stalin
- Nancy Pelosi

Worth Noting: If you haven't yet read on any of the other types you may not notice the distinctions of the famous ENTJs. Compared with other types, ENTJs excel in business and political positions and are natural Executives. This makes perfect sense since ENTJs are born leaders with a strong drive.

GOING DEEPER EXERCISE

Of the famous ENTJs on this list, which are you most familiar with?

_____

_____

_____

_____

_____

What are some common elements you notice? These could be specific personality traits or characteristics. It could also include actions they have taken or tough decisions they have made. For example: Going against the grain or choosing to follow a passion.

_____

_____

_____

_____

_____

YOUR SECRET WEAPONS

(Aka your unique strengths)

In my own life I have found no greater success secret than discovering, *and applying*, my strengths.

When we are young we're often taught that we need to be good at many things. For example, schools are based on your average grade and most parents which much prefer their child have a smooth report card of all B+s then two A+s and two C-s.

The real world doesn't reward the well-rounded individual, at least not exceptionally well. Those who receive the greatest rewards are those who focus on their strengths and ignore all else. Think of people like Arnold Schwarzenegger, Steve Jobs and Oprah Winfrey.

Does anyone *really* care if Oprah is bad at math, if Arnold has trouble managing his personal life or if Steve Jobs was a bit of an ass to employees from time to time?

Nope. No one cares because each of these Greats focused on their strengths and created an extraordinary life for themselves.

Oprah (an ENFJ) harnessed her empathy and ability to build trust and bond with people to create incredible interviews and connect with her audience.

Arnold (an INTJ) used his focus, discipline, and strategic thinking to achieve incredible goals in fitness, performing and politics despite being the underdog in almost everything he ever did.

Steve Jobs (an ISTP) kept his energy focused on his creative and visual strengths. His visions were so clear, and his innovations so impressive, that his social graces didn't matter.

Now, as you read on you will discover the unique strengths closely linked to ENTJs. While you read this remember that these are the strengths that come naturally to you, but you still need to develop and fine-tune them if you want to thrive.

ENTJ's strengths revolve around their future orientation (vision), objective decision making abilities and strong internal drive to translate their goals into reality.

AN ENTJ's SECRET WEAPONS

- An incredible ability to set a goal and go after it without many, if any, emotional hiccups or personal challenges getting in the way.

- An ability to synthesize new information and ideas and apply them to their current goals. This makes them excellent strategists in business, financial and even social situations.

- An ability to easily turn the understanding of a situation into a plan of action.

- Overall, ENTJs want to do what is right. They value social order, government, and things working as they should. They are happy to pay their taxes and follow the rules and expect others to do the same.

- Excellent organizational and time management abilities. Couple this with their strong drive to succeed, and you can understand why ENTJs are very good at achieving their goals.

- ENTJs' objective way of seeing things and organizational skills translate into an excellent ability to make and manage money.

- They are great verbal communicators and are quick on their feet. They can answer a question or rebuttal a joke without too much effort. This also makes them excellent debaters.

28

- ENTJs can quickly read a room or social situation and assert themselves as the leader in the room.
- ENTJs are driven and take a "can and will do" approach to everything they do. This makes competitive sports and business environments alike very enjoyable for them.
- ENTJs can be objective and think through a situation or decision based on the facts alone.
- Highly Developed ENTJs Will Enjoy Even More Super Powers:
- A decent ability to understand other peoples' feelings and needs, as well as a desire to understand the differences between these feelings and needs and the ENTJ's own.
- Gain the ability to slow down and enjoy the present moment. ENTJs aren't born with an "Off Button"; it times time and matures for them to develop an appreciation of the slower aspects of life.
- On a broader level, this may show itself in an ENTJ Senior Manager finally starting to take all their allotted vacation time each year, even if it means their performance numbers may suffer a tiny bit.
- The ability to coach others to overcome their challenges and move towards their goals.
- The ability to be a team player and include others in their decision making as well as a share of the credit and rewards that come from them.
- A desire to, and talent for, taking on social issues and working for the greater good.

In summary, a developed ENTJ can be:

- Goal Oriented
- Very Driven and Determined
- Future Oriented
- Persistent

- Great With Money
- Well Read (Values Knowledge)
- A Powerful Leader
- Self-Confident
- Decisive
- Well Liked, Social
- Highly Organized
- Orderly and Structured
- On Time
- Insightful
- Creative
- Intelligent
- Logical
- Focused
- Quick
- Caring
- Intuitive
- Inspiring

Keys To Using Your Strengths as an ENTJ

- Make time to spend with people and allow your mind to relax. This is not only good for your body and mind; it's good for your goals as well. Often it is during this "down time" when the best ideas are formulated.
- Focus on goals that will bring a balanced happiness to your life and are inclusive of home and family.
- Realize you're unique among most groups and learn to accept others (and their weaknesses).

In this and future chapters you will discover "Going Deeper" exercises. These are designed to help you better understand and apply the chapter's content. If you're like me you may want to write your answers down. When you bought this book you also got access to a companion workbook you can print and then fill in with your answers as you go. You can download the workbook for free at:

www.DreamsAroundTheWorld.com/thrive

GOING DEEPER EXERCISE

Of the strengths listed above, which most jump out at you as strengths of your own?

_____

_____

_____

_____

_____

What are 3 strengths listed above that you know you have but are not actively using in your life, at least not as much as you know you should?

_____

_____

_____

_____

_____

How could you apply these strengths more frequently?

_____

_____

_____

_____

YOUR KRYPTONITE
(Aka your potential weaknesses)

You didn't think I was going to stop at your strengths did you? As much as I say *focus on your strengths* it is still important to be aware of your weaknesses, even if it is just so you can more easily ignore them.

Below you will find a list of weaknesses, or challenges, common amongst ENTJs. As with strengths, this is not a definitive list and do not take it as a prescription for how ENTJs have to be.

Sometimes I will see posts in a Facebook group for a specific type where people seem overly proud of their type challenges. I remember one post on an ENFP group making light at how the poster had been unable to tidy their room in 4 days. While it was good for a "we've all been there" chuckle, I did find myself turned off at what a chaotic life this person must have. They have chosen to neither fix their weakness (by developing their self-discipline and follow through) nor embrace it (by hiring a maid). Instead, they have chosen to suffer what they described as 4 days of agony simply trying to clean a room.

So if some of these weaknesses don't really resonate with you, **good**. Ignore them and don't assume you should be weak in that area if you're not. If you do connect with some of the weaknesses, take it as an opportunity to either work to improve that area of yourself, or to accept the weakness and find a solution so you don't have to deal with it.

Many of the ENTJs' challenges tend to revolve around their dominant function (extroverted thinking) being overdeveloped to the point where it takes over. This leads to the other functions, such as how they process internally (introverted intuition), being largely ignored and life being experienced very objectively based on what is first experienced in a situation. This cuts the ENTJ off from a substantial amount of insight and intuition they would otherwise have available about situations and people.

As you read these, remember they are only a result of an underdeveloped personality and can easily be overcome by developing weaker areas. Think of each point as a potential diagnosis you would get from a Doctor for an easy to cure condition. The first step to treating it is awareness followed by treatment.

COMMON KRYPTONITE FOR THE ENTJ

Before they fully develop their personalities, some ENTJs *may* recognize some of the following weaknesses:

- Getting stuck on little details of a plan and losing sight of the big picture and overall plan.
- Pushing themselves too hard to meet very high personal expectations or neglecting to take care of their own needs when going after an ambitious goal.
- One ENTJ told me he constantly feels like there is a Dragon breathing fire at his feet and if he stops for a moment too long he'll be swallowed up in flames.
- Tied to the point above, ENTJs may confuse the natural limits of their abilities with a weakness they need to fix or overcome. In reality, we all have limits in certain areas.
- The goal should be to maximize our potential while focusing on our strengths.
- ENTJs can become almost dictatorial. When this happens they will see their way of doing things as the right and only way for them to be done. This can be made worse by the ENTJ's rather strong and forceful personality.
- Taking things too personally. Despite being "objective" themselves, ENTJs will often take someone's disagreement

with their own rather rational beliefs as a personal rejection.

- Relative to other types, the ENTJs rarely use their "feeling" function and thus it is underdeveloped.
- When an ENTJ faces a situation where they're forced to express or confront their feelings they may become angered or throw an emotional tantrum.
- This regression to a childish state may be a reflection of the underdeveloped state or level of their feeling function.
- An inability to understand the needs of other people when they differ from their own. They may not understand why someone has difficulty with confrontation or fails to meet their sales goals.
  They may miss the opportunity to nurture talents in others because they have trouble seeing the differences between them or understanding the feelings of others.
- They may fail to utilize the knowledge or abilities that those around them bring to the table.
- For instance, they may presume that the quietest person in a meeting, let's say an INFJ, doesn't have anything to offer to the discussion. In reality, many types are just quieter or may feel too intimidated by the ENTJ to express a different opinion.

OVERCOMING YOUR WEAKNESSES

Many of the ENTJ's weaknesses share a single root cause. If they do not develop their secondary function, introverted intuition, ENTJs' other functions will be dominated by their extroverted thinking function.

If they do not develop their secondary function, "introverted intuition", the ENTJ will see the world only in black and white. The problem with this intellectual only view of the world is that people and relationships don't function in black and white. There isn't always a clear right and wrong, and even if there is, it often doesn't matter when it comes to personal relationships and peoples' feelings.

One way to develop this habit is to practice focusing on other people and new points of view. Read autobiographies and stories. Take the time to understand why other people act how they do. This includes understanding their value system, which is not inherently any better or worse than your own.

During day-to-day interactions with others, ENTJs will benefit from taking time to ask questions about how other people feel. "Why do you do it that way?" or "how does it make you feel when _____?" are great ones to start with.

It may feel weird at first, but you'll be surprised at what you learn. For example, for years I did not watch, read or listen to the news. An ENTJ friend of mine thought it was insane that I never watched the news until one day I explain my reasons to him. I'm an ENFP and, at least at the time, my emotional state was easily influenced. I found that not only was most news a waste of my time, but it also left me feeling weak, helpless or just cynical about the world.

After I explained how I felt inside, it sounded like my choice to skip the morning news made a lot more sense to him. As an added bonus, just asking people about their feelings will show you care and make other people feel good.

To develop your introverted intuition function, try this: Whenever you are faced with an important decision, take as long as possible to make it. Sit (or walk) with your thoughts. Allow yourself to experience the images and thoughts that come up for you. Try and push aside the ones that immediately pop up, as they are products of your extroverted thinking and initial judgements. Push them aside and make room for your intuition to go to work. Think through each new idea and allow your intuition to go play with it.

At first this may be difficult, like the first time you swung a tennis racquet or tried to use a smartphone. Stick with it; very quickly you'll feel your intuition growing and this exercise becoming much easier.

GOING DEEPER EXERCISE

Of the weaknesses listed above, which 3 do you most recognize in yourself?

_____

_____

_____

_____

What are 3 weaknesses listed above that you know are having a significant negative impact on your success?

_____

_____

_____

_____

How could you reduce the impact these weaknesses have on your life, by either learning to overcome them, or eliminating the activities that bring them to the surface? What steps will you take this week to do so?

_____

_____

_____

_____

Note: If you're like me you may want to write your answers down. When you bought this book you also got access to a companion workbook you can print and then fill in with your answers as you go. You can download the workbook for free at:

www.DreamsAroundTheWorld.com/thrive

IDEAL CAREER OPTIONS FOR AN ENTJ

If you gave a Myers-Briggs test to a group of a few hundred people from the same profession you would see a very clear pattern.

An Accountant in my martial arts class told me that of 600 Chartered Accountants who took the Myers-Briggs test at his firm, he was one of only 3 people who didn't score the same type.

This happens for two reasons:

1) Selection Bias: People with the personality type for accounting will tend to do well in related tasks and receive hints that that kind of work is right for them. They may especially enjoy numbers, spreadsheets etc.

2) Survival Bias: Those with the personality type for accounting are most likely to pass the vigorous tests and internships required to become a Charted Accountant.

We are actually much better at finding the right path for us than we give ourselves credit for. In almost every profession, there is a significantly higher percentage of those "typed" to excel in it than random chance would have.

Yet, many people still slip through the cracks, or spend decades searching for that perfect career before finding it.

This chapter will help you avoid the cracks and stop wasting your precious time. Below you'll find a comprehensive list of careers ENTJs tend to be drawn to and succeed in.

There are many more career options beyond this list that I have seen in other books and intentionally not included here. These include "good" options that an ENTJ could easily do and succeed in, but would not be as happy or fulfilled as they would in another profession where they could use their real strengths.

I have included only the options I believe ENTJs have an upper hand in *and* the highest likelihood to find fulfillment and success. There are always other options, but why swim upstream if you don't need to right?

TO BE MOST SUCCESSFUL, AN ENTJ SHOULD FOCUS ON WORK THAT:

- Allows the ENTJ to utilize their natural abilities to organize, lead, and drive projects forward.
- Happens within a fair and standardized work environment and includes fair compensation that rewards hard work and contribution. There should be an established set of criteria used to judge performance so that everyone is compensated fairly (and predictably) based on their contributions.
- Incorporates a high degree of learning. ENTJs are always striving to improve their aptitude and add to their skillset. One way they do this is through new information and experiences.
- Doesn't involve repetitive tasks or require the ENTJ to intervene in interpersonal conflicts or day-to-day people problems.
- Allows them to produce work based on their own (usually very high) standards instead of the personal opinions of others.
- Takes place in an exciting and competitive environment involving important people and decisions.

- Is in the public eye where the ENTJ may feel admired for the work they do and be recognized for their accomplishments.
- Allows the ENTJ to set their own goals while leading and managing their team to accomplish them.
- Lets the ENTJ spend time with a diverse group of people, including goal-oriented people they admire and respect. Of particular interest to the ENTJ is spending time around powerful individuals they aspire to be like and have the opportunity to grow their networks (and own power).
- Includes a variety of people, projects and challenges so the day is filled with excitement and mental stimulation.
- Provides a chance to see and experience the results of their vision and hard work.
- Acknowledges and rewards original thought, proficiency and accomplishment with credit going to the ENTJ for their contributions.

POPULAR PROFESSIONS FOR ENTJS

Business

- Executive (C Level)
- Executive (Vice President)
- Senior manager
- Sales manager
- Sales Consultation (Business to Business)
- Marketing manager
- Network integration specialist
- Information services (sales)
- Advertising account manager
- Marketing executive: radio/TV/cable broadcast
- Media planner/buyer
- International sales and marketing
- Franchise owner
- Sales manager: pharmaceuticals
- University administrator
- Managing editor
- Theater producer
- Police supervisor
- Association manager & adviser
- Program director
- Project manager
- Real estate manager

Finance and Consulting

- Business consultant
- Management consultant
- Educational consultant
- Program designer
- Management trainer
- Logistics consultant
- Management consultant
- Corporate team trainer
- Political consultant
- Corporate finance attorney
- International banker
- Economist
- Treasurer, controller, CFO
- Venture capitalist
- Personal financial planner
- Economic analyst
- Mortgage broker
- Credit investigator
- Stockbroker
- Investment banker

Technology and Computers

- Network administrator
- Systems administrator
- Local area network administrator
- Robotics network manager
- Database administrator
- Systems analyst
- Project manager
- Engagement manager

Professional

- Attorney
- Judge
- Science or social sciences teacher
- Psychologist
- Chemical engineer
- Intellectual property attorney
- Biomedical engineer
- Psychiatrist
- Environmental engineer
- Attorney
- Political scientist
- Pathologist
- Pilot

GOING DEEPER EXERCISE

Read through the list above and answer the following questions.

1) Which 5-10 careers jump out at you as something you'd enjoy doing?

_____

_____

_____

_____

_____

2) Thinking back to the sections on strengths, what do you notice about the list of careers? What strengths might contribute to success in these careers?

_____

_____

_____

_____

_____

THRIVING AT WORK

There is an astronomical difference between a job you're good at and a career you love and in which you thrive.

While some people are fine just getting by, people like you and I sure aren't. This section will help you thrive at work.

3 Foundations For Thriving At Work

1) Be aware of your strengths and weaknesses and be selective of the work you do. Be honest in job interviews about where you excel as well as where you struggle.

2) When in a job, take this same honest approach with your supervisor. Explain that you aren't being lazy; rather you feel you could deliver much more *value* to the company by focusing on your strengths.

3) At least once per week, if not daily, stop for a few minutes and ask yourself if you're working in your strengths or struggling in your weaknesses. Remember, you have unique and valuable gifts...but only if you make the effort to use them and avoid getting trapped in the wrong kind of work.

SECRET WEAPONS AT WORK

When it comes to your work, be sure to tap into these work related strengths for ENTJs:

- Have the ability to see the big picture and understand the consequences of specific approaches or actions.
- Great communication social skills, especially when used in a sales environment.
- The ability to commit and make 'final' decisions (decisiveness) and solid organizational skills.

- High levels of confidence and a natural leadership ability. They have the courage to make decisions and take action.
- Naturally organized in all areas including time (schedules), space (environment) and finances.
- Enjoys challenges and competition. Very comfortable with confrontation whether it is a heated negotiation, a sales meeting, or having to fire someone.
- Can be objective and think through an issue without taking it personally or letting their own values bias their decision.
- Independent. Able to jump into a project, take risks, and just do it without much supervision or guidance. This includes having confidence in their ideas and the courage to move forward with them.
- Interested in systems and determining the best way to get things done. Couple this with their strong drive to succeed, and you can understand why ENTJs are very good at achieving their goals.
- Is a natural problem solver, always able to come up with a creative solution.
- Internal drive to be productive, achieve goals, and excel at whatever they do.
- Generally, they're great with technology.

KRYPTONITE AT WORK

To maximize their success, ENTJs should be aware of some challenges they face at work. ENTJs will not always, but **may:**

- They may have trouble working with people they see as incompetent.
- Not interested in the mundane details of a project (although they have no problem "following through" in general).
- Be impatient with those who aren't as "quick" as them and tend to "ponder" things.

- Be stubborn. Once they flex their "decisive" muscle and make a decision they are reluctant to step backwards and revisit it.
- Can be overpowering or just straight intimidating to those around them, especially to those with a dislike of conflict.
- Tendency to fix what isn't broken. In other words, they may try and improve things that really don't need to be improved (or at least it shouldn't be their priority).
- Can be too tough on others. This includes placing their own high standards on others and neglecting to give praise and appreciation to those they work with.
- They may give work too much priority in relation to their home life and neglect other important aspects of their lives.

RICH AND HAPPY RELATIONSHIPS

Whoever said opposites attract never met an ENFP + ISTJ couple.

Sure, you want a partner who complements your strengths and weaknesses, but most of us also want someone who understands us: someone with whom we can express our opinions and ideas and be understood.

In this section we'll start with a discussion on what ENTJs are like in relationships. Then we'll look at the most common personality types ENTJs are happy with. Lastly, we will end with some advice on creating and maintaining successful relationships as an ENTJ, and *with* an ENTJ.

ENTJS' IDEAL MATCHES

A note on compatibility: There is no be all and end all. The information on type compatibility is either based on theory or surveys, neither of which will ever provide a universal rule.

NT (rational) types find the greatest relationship *satisfaction* dating NFs. This is likely because they can share a common way of thinking about the world. With that said, the most compatible match for ENTJs are INFPs and INTPs.

Ultimately, the two individuals involved, and their desire to grow and work to create an incredible relationship, will have the biggest determination of their success together. The one incompatibility that I've noticed time and time again is between Intuitives (Ns) and Sensors (Ss). I think this is because these two groups have fundamentally different ways of interacting with the world and often have trouble understanding one another.

In my own experience in romantic relationships, friendships, and business partnerships, I (a strong Intuitive – ENFP), have always run into trouble with those who rate highly on the Sensor mode of being. With all that said, ENTJs are the one Intuitive type that rates about the same marital satisfaction with both Intuitives and Sensors.

Beyond that, it's all up in the air. Generally, for organization sake, I would suggest that Ps match with a J. The P will benefit from the J's structure and organization, and the J will benefit from the P's creativity and spontaneity.

TIPS FOR DATING AS AN ENTJ

- You may set very high expectations for yourself and your partner. Just remember that everyone is human, and no partner or relationship will be perfect so don't be too hard on your partner, or yourself.
- ENTJs are driven to succeed and have a tendency to emphasize the "work" part of work-life balance. When looking for a lifelong mate, ask yourself: "Will this person be happy supporting me during long work hours or periods of stress?" To avoid conflict, you need a confident partner who will give you emotional support and time to be free to do your own thing.
- You most likely desire a clear, beautiful, and well-maintained home. You're also likely to be the main income earner in your household. Being the 21st century, it's important you discuss this with any potential partners. Are they on board for a traditional relationship where one party works and the other manages the home?
- ENTJs can be intimidating and over bearing at times. A more sensitive partner may not feel comfortable expressing themselves or confronting you on certain issues. They may put up with this situation but not actually be happy and possibly even suffering a lot of emotional distress because of it. It's very important you frequently

make time to discuss your partner's feelings or select a partner who shares your rational (nt) traits.

TIPS FOR DATING AN ENTJ

- While they are usually the most powerful person in the room, when it comes to emotions, ENTJs can feel inferior and very sensitive. Help them along by providing opportunities to casually discuss feelings or situations without judgement.
- Take time to express your emotions and explain how certain words or situations make you feel. Your ENTJ partner may care but just genuinely not understand how you feel.
- While they can be intimidating or overbearing, ENTJs don't always see themselves as such. In fact, they love it when people are able to go "toe to toe" with them in debate and hold their own. If you're someone comfortable with confrontation and debate this can be a good thing and an opportunity to flex your own debater muscle.
- On the other hand, if you're genuinely averse to conflict you need to consider this before committing to a life with an ENTJ. Will you be happy taking the backseat on decisions and follower role in the relationship or are you someone who has to take the lead or at least share the Captain's seat?
- ENTJs are prone to sentimental streaks of emotions, kind words or gifts. They may also feel a little awkward about them, believing that emotions make them vulnerable or weak. So, if your ENTJ seems to be on a sentimental streak be gentle with them and avoid any kind of criticism.
- ENTJs are exceptionally well organized and great with finances. If you want to build a life with an ENTJ, they will most likely take charge of this area of your lives together.

- ENTJs tend to see conflict as a problem they can solve with logic. This might play out much like the typical comedic scene between a man and a woman, with the man trying to solve emotional problems in the same fashion he would repair a car. Be aware that this is simply how your partner's mind is wired and isn't a reflection of their level of caring. They care about you; they just try and solve problems rationally. Make an effort to explain how you feel and how what they say impacts you, as they might not actually know.

- ENTJs are very driven to achieve their goals and tend to focus their energy on their work, which they see as the path to security and happiness. To women, this can make them very attractive as powerful and successful men, but men who may not have the time or emotions needed to satisfy a more demanding partner.

To learn more about how all the types relate and interact, download the free compatibility chart at:

www.DreamsAroundTheWorld.com/thrive

QUOTES FOR THE ENJOYMENT OF ENTJS ONLY

Here you'll find a collection of fun, inspiring, and relatable quotes for ENTJs, from famous or accomplished ENTJs.

"I think in life we want to challenge ourselves."

-Charlize Theron

"My life isn't focused on results. My life is really focused on the process of doing all the things I'm doing, from work to relationships to friendships to charitable work."

-George Clooney

"It is better to create than to learn! Creating is the essence of life."

-Julius Caesar

"My nature is that I have to excite myself with a big challenge."

-Garry Kasparov

"To wear your heart on your sleeve isn't a very good plan; you should wear it inside, where it functions best."

-Margaret Thatcher

"An organization's ability to learn, and translate that learning into action rapidly, is the ultimate competitive advantage."

-Jack Welch

"At the end of the day, it's all about money."

-Garry Kasparov

"I actually thought that it would be a little confusing during the same period of your life to be in one meeting when you're trying to make money, and then go to another meeting where you're giving it away. I mean is it gonna erode your ability, you know, to make money? Are you gonna somehow get confused about what you're trying to do?"

-Bill Gates

"Pleasure in the job puts perfection in the work."

-Aristotle

"I think it's still hard for me to turn down work if it's really good because for so many years I was so desperate to get a job and couldn't and so it's kind of an anathema for me to turn down work."

-Matt Damon

"Building a professional relationship on respect as opposed to affection is a very good idea. Running your art projects the way you'd run a dry-cleaning business is also a really good idea. You shouldn't go into work like you're going on a date, like you're hanging out with friends."

-Penn Jillette

"As a rule, what is out of sight disturbs men's minds more seriously than what they see"

-Julius Caesar

"Luck is statistics taken personally."

-Penn Jillette

"Knowing yourself is the beginning of all wisdom."

-Aristotle

"No one is so brave that he is not disturbed by some unexpected twist in his plan."

-Julius Caesar

"Sometimes something worth doing is worth overdoing."

-David Letterman

"Valid criticism is doing you a favor."

-Carl Sagan

KEYS TO WEALTH, HEALTH, HAPPINESS AND SUCCESS

I hope this book has provided some insights into how you can succeed in the most important areas of your life.

In this last section, I'd like to share ten strategies to remember that will help you create a balanced and happy life. If you apply them, these strategies will help you enjoy more wealth, health and happiness in your life.

1. Learn how to slow down and enjoy the present moment. ENTJs aren't born with an "Off Button"; it takes time and maturity for them to develop an appreciation of the slower aspects of life.

2. Speaking of downtime, make time to spend quality time in a relaxing environment and give your mind permission to turn off. Often it is during this "down time" when your best ideas are formulated.

3. ENTJs must follow strengths and do work that is aligned with their abilities. Take on work that will reward you for your ability to create strategic plans, lead, and go after your goals.

4. Be accountable and take personal responsibility. It is important to be aware of your weaknesses but do not use this knowledge as an excuse. Never blame others. When you blame others for your circumstances you give away the power to change them. Take responsibility for your life and you give yourself the power to change it.

5. ENTJs really dislike repetitive work so stick to big picture and "project based" work and leave the admin to others.

6. Learn to understand others. You have a unique and wonderful way of looking at the world...but it is one of many and no more right than any others. Learn to understand how other people see the world and your influence will increase while the amount of conflict in your world decreases.

7. ENTJs are often far too hard on themselves and those close to them. You have very high standards for yourself and that's good, but comparing yourself or others to a lofty vision can lead to harsh and unfair judgements that won't contribute to your success. Take time to review accomplishments, progress and positive traits.

8. Make an effort to praise and show appreciation for those around you. You may be very confident and self-assured, but not everyone is. A few kind words from you can go a long way in motivating those you work with and lifting the spirits of the people you care about.

9. Focus on goals that will bring a balanced happiness to your life.

10. Make an effort to develop an understanding of other peoples' feelings and needs, as well as the differences between these feelings and needs and your own.

NEXT STEPS

To help you get the most from this book I have created a collection of free extras to support you along the way. If you haven't already, take a few minutes now to request the free bonuses; you already paid for them when you bought this book. To download these, simply visit the special section of my website: www.dreamsaroundtheworld.com/thrive

There you will be asked to enter your email address so I can send you the "Thriving Bonus Pack". You'll receive:

- A 5-part mini-course (delivered via email) with tips on how to adjust your life so you can best make use of your strengths.
- A compatibility chart showing how you are most likely to relate to the other 15 personality types. You'll discover which types are most compatible with you and which types will likely lead to headaches.
- A PDF workbook which complements this book. It's formatted to be printed, so you can fill in your answers to the exercises in each chapter as you go.

To download the Thriving Bonus Pack, visit:

www.DreamsAroundTheWorld.com/thrive

Books In The Thrive Personality Type Series

The ENFP Superhero : Harness your gifts, Inspire others and Thrive as an ENFP

Or just visit Amazon and search for "ENFP". Then look for the book by Dan Johnston.

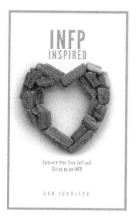

INFP Inspired: Embrace your true self and thrive as an INFP

Or just visit Amazon and search for "INFP". Then look for the book by Dan Johnston.

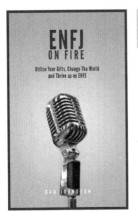

ENFJ on fire: Utilize your gifts, Change the world and thrive as an ENFJ

Or just visit Amazon and search for "ENFJ". Then look for the book by Dan Johnston.

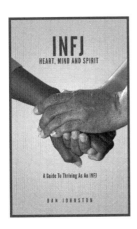

INFJ, Heart, Mind and Spirit: A Guide to thriving as an INFJ

Or just visit Amazon and search for "INFJ". Then look for the book by Dan Johnston.

The Well Rounded ENTJ: Find more harmony, Improve relationships and thrive as a natural leader

Or just visit Amazon and search for "ENTJ". Then look for the book by Dan Johnston.

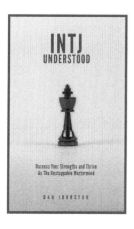

INTJ Understood: Harness your strengths and thrive as the unstoppable mastermind

Or just visit Amazon and search for "INTJ". Then look for the book by Dan Johnston.

The ENTP Plan: Invent yourself, make progress and thrive as the charming and visionary ENTP

Or just visit Amazon and search for "ENTP". Then look for the book by Dan Johnston.

INTP: Utilize your strengths, solve life's problems and thrive as the genius thinker type INTP

Or just visit Amazon and search for "INTP". Then look for the book by Dan Johnston.

Thrive Series Collections

The Idealists: Learning To Thrive As, and With, ENFPs, INFPs, ENFJs and INFJs (A Collection Of Four Books From The Thrive Series)

The Rationals: Learning To Thrive As, and With, The INTJ, ENTJ, INTP and ENTP Personality Types (A Collection of Four Books From The Thrive Series)

About The Author

Dan Johnston is a #1 international best-selling author, speaker, coach, and recognized expert in the fields of confidence, psychology and personal transformation. As a coach, one of his specialties is helping clients discover their natural talents, apply them to their true purpose and create a plan of action to live the life of their dreams.

Dan publishes new videos weekly on his YouTube Channel. Here you will hundreds of videos on psychology and personality type.

This is the best place to catch Dan's latest content: www.YouTube.com/DreamsAroundTheWorld/

If you prefer to listen, check our Dan's podcast here: www.DreamsAroundTheWorld.com/podcast

To learn more about Dan Johnston and his coaching services visit:
www.DreamsAroundTheWorld.com/coaching

For articles, interviews and resources on entrepreneurship, pursuing your passions, travel and creating the life of your dreams, visit Dreams Around The World and subscribe to the "The Life Design Approach":

www.DreamsAroundTheWorld.com

Find more books By Dan Johnston on his Amazon Author Central Pages:
Amazon.com:
http://www.amazon.com/author/danjohnston

Amazon.co.uk:
http://www.amazon.co.uk/-/e/B00E1DO6OS

Never Settle – A Short Article

This is an article I wrote for revolution. It is on a topic near and dear to my heart. I've included it in this book to let you learn a little bit more about me, and hopefully to inspire you to think big and always go after your dreams. Dan.

Never Settle

"That is seriously your life? You are literally living the dream. That's insane."

I've grown to expect this every time I tell someone about my fairy-tale of a life. But trust me, it wasn't always this way.

A lot people put off travel, passions and happiness until some distant future point; be it the sale of their business, a promotion, or retirement. I used to be one of them.

I owned my own business and I worked like a dog with the dream of one day "making it". Then I could make happiness a priority. I sacrificed friendships, health, family and travel opportunities all because I had to work harder for "just a little while longer." I just needed to "make it" and then things would be different. Then I could I finally start enjoying life.

That was until my business imploded and left me completely, and I mean completely, broke. To get it started I needed to co-sign all the business loans and other liabilities, and so when the business failed so did I. Rock bottom occurred. Public failure. Massive financial stress. All that sort of good stuff.

I can actually remember one night when I was terrified my date would show up hungry because so much as grabbing a pizza together would mean I couldn't afford pasta and milk the following week. I now refer to this time of my life as my "Pursuit of Happyness" phase.

But life must go on, right? What was I going to do, marry a government employee, move to Idaho and get a job as an accountant? Not in this lifetime. And for the record, what the hell does "making it" even mean?!

Fast-forward about 10 months and I'm working as a freelancer and still struggling. It's Saturday evening and the weather is just miserable. Dark clouds, drizzling rain, cold enough to be uncomfortable yet not like a romantic Christmas cold you get bundled up for and almost enjoy. I was at home thinking about my situation and suddenly was overcome with emotions. Where was the light at the end of the tunnel? Something has to change or I'm not going to make it.

I knew I needed to make a serious change in my life because I couldn't handle the stress much longer. The clear decision was to "Call It Quits" and move back home for a bit. Start applying for jobs, save up a little money, and start rebuilding my life.

Lucky for me the windows were fogged that night and I wasn't seeing clearly. Fuelled by half a bottle of red wine and a desire to live true to myself and my word, I booked a one-way ticket to Costa Rica.

Two weeks later, with less than a month's living expenses in the bank and no steady income I was off to the airport and I had no idea what awaited me on the other side.

It was a huge risk...and it paid off.

The change of scener reset my emotional clock. The sun beamed energy into my heart and soul. My business grew, like really grew. Four weeks after arriving in Costa Rica, I called my little brother and surprised him with a plane ticket to come visit me the following week. And yes, I could now afford to treat my date to a pepperoni pizza.

This was early 2012. Since then I've lived in 5 countries, heading towards my 6th next week (Barcelona, Spain). I've crossed countless items from my bucket list including driving a Lamborghini on my birthday, speaking Spanish, playing with a baby monkey, learning to surf and driving a Hank Moody inspired Porsche up Highway 101.

When things got hard I had plenty of opportunities to raise the white flag. To retreat. To turn my back on the life I really wanted.

I'm sure you'll have the same opportunities. Ignore them.

Don't ever, ever think going for it, going after what you really want, will be easy.

But it will always, always be worth it.

For More Visit:

www.DreamsAroundTheWorld.com

Exclusive Reader-Only Bonuses:

To help you get the most from this book I have created a collection of free extras to support you along the way.

When you visit the site below you will be able to download a printable workbook to record your reflections and answers to the end of chapter exercises.

You will also receive free enrollment in a Five-Part E-Course on personality psychology delivered by e-mail. The training is packed with tips, strategies, advice and additional resources.

Through the five lessons, you will learn how to implement what you have learnt about your personality type, including:

- How To Learn From Your Mistakes and Gain Experience Fast
- Why You Must, and How You Can, Become The Best In The World
- How to Overcome Your Weak Spots
- How to Put Your Strengths into Action and Achieve Your Highest Potential.
- How To Pay It Forward By Understanding Those Around You and Helping Them Become Their Best Selves

Both are yours free, a special thank you for my readers.

To receive your free companion course and workbook, visit:

www.dreamsaroundtheworld.com/thrive

Made in the USA
Columbia, SC
18 September 2020